Aerial photo of Aldridge Gardens, 1985.

A Garden of Destiny

By Eddie Aldridge

The founder of Aldridge Botanical Gardens in Hoover, Alabama, shares his personal story—from his family's beginnings in the horticultural business through the development and nurturing of an important public garden.

Terry ~ GibeLA
THANKS for your support
We hope you enjoy our journey
of destiny

Eddie J Aldridge

This book was written in Alabama. Edited in Alabama. Designed in Alabama. Printed and published in Alabama and the entire proceeds will benefit Aldridge Gardens in Hoover, Alabama.

Library of Congress Control Number: 2008939842

ISBN: 1-59421-049-7

Published by Seacoast Publishing, Inc.
Post Office Box 26492
Birmingham, AL 35260

Book Design by Elizabeth Chick
Cover Photo by Larry Gay

To obtain copies of this book contact:
Aldridge Botanical Gardens
3530 Lorna Road
Hoover, Alabama 35216
(205) 682-8019

d Destiny: a seemingly inevitable or necessary succession of events

Every good and perfect gift is from above, coming down from the father of the Heavenly lights, who does not change like shifting shadows.

James 1:17

thanks...

I would like to offer a special thanks to the city of Hoover—beginning with the 1995 administration that started the gardens through all succeeding administrations— for their outstanding support.

Thank you to all our board members from the very beginning until today for all their contributions to the gardens.

Special thanks to my wife Kay. Without her many hours of computer work on this publication, it would not have been possible.

Thank you to Lynn Carter for patiently editing this publication.

And thank you for the help and efforts of Janis Bailey and Seacoast Publishing for making our life easier.

— Eddie Aldridge

This publication is in memory of my parents, Loren L. Aldridge
and Zeta McTyeire Aldridge, and my brother, Loren McTyeire Aldridge.
This garden is named in their memory.

Mr. and Mrs. Aldridge, Eddie and Mac, about 1950.

My Mother and Father

Loren L. Aldridge and Zeta McTyeire Aldridge

Mr. and Mrs. Aldridge.

i'm not sure what my father's ambition was when he was young, but he excelled at everything he attempted to do in his life. He excelled in high school, through college in the early 1920s, and in every phase of his life. My father was the best teacher I had during my lifetime, and, before he died in 1978, he provided the vision for this garden.

L. L. ALDRIDGE, Α Γ Ρ, Α Φ Ε, Φ Δ Γ, Φ Κ Φ . Boaz
Agricultural Education

Spades; Blue Key; Ag. Club, (3, 2, 1); Vice-President, (1); Y. M. C., Lieutenant, (3), Captain, (2), Major, (1); Business Manager Alabama Farmer, (1); Wilsonian Literary Society, (2, 1), Treasurer, (2); Rat Football; Scrub Football, (3, 2); Varsity Football, (1); Class Football, (4, 3, 2); Captain, (2); Founders Club; Distinction, (2).

A more popular man than "Percy" has never graced our campus. Such popularity was well deserved and we are certain that it will remain with him when he leaves.

1926 API, Alabama Polytechnic Institute, Yearbook.

Two of the original cuttings made from the surviving cutting at the McTyeire-Aldridge Cemetery lot at Cedar Hill Cemetery in Bessemer, AL.

My mother, like my father, earned her college degree in the early twenties. It was rare for couples to both have college degrees at that time. How lucky I was to be blessed with parents who never faltered in offering me guidance, teaching, and inspiration. While I never felt that I totally lived up to the example they set for me, I have sure tried.

Fall Ginkgo leaves.

Lower end of Kay's Woodland Stream.

*a*As I sit today at the center of Aldridge Botanical Gardens overlooking the beauty of the surrounding thirty acres, I begin to reflect on my life's work and on the twists and turns that have led me to this moment of peace and reflection. As I recall my family's beginnings and growth in the nursery business and my own years

Eddie on a bench donated by Richard Tasich in honor of Dr. Betty Lee.

of work and struggles, I am struck by how so many decisions seemed to lead to a positive outcome. So many happy coincidences, so many lucky decisions that led to the development of these gardens. In spite of some personal setbacks, I seemed to be always moving in a positive direction that could not be explained just by coincidence or luck.

House on the lake in the Fall.

Winston Churchill once said that free will and predestination are identical. He believed that he made choices and these choices were fulfilling destiny because man's choice is the vehicle of God's unfolding plan. I too believe that the choices I made were guided by a higher power and the results achieved are proof of a higher plan.

As I overlook this beautiful acreage, now dedicated to the enjoyment and education of all who care to come, I truly believe that destiny was an important part of this successful story. I hope my readers will enjoy the highs and lows of my journey as much as I have enjoyed living it.

In the Beginning

*t*o tell the story of Aldridge Gardens, I must begin with a brief history of our family business and how it started. My parents, Zeta McTyeire and Loren L. Aldridge, met as schoolteachers in 1926 at Bessemer High School. My mother was an English teacher and my father taught science. He had graduated that year from Auburn with a degree in agriculture. My parents were married on Christmas day of

Spring-fed lake and company headquarters in Bessemer.

Eddie and Mac on Daisy Mae, about 1937.

that same year. After teaching about three years, they decided to start a small business growing and selling cut flowers and other plants. They bought some already constructed greenhouses from West Birmingham and had them erected on land they had bought from my grandfather, Dr. R. P. McTyeire. And so the family gardening business began in the late 1920s. Most of the plants they sold were cut flowers to the florist trade, mainly in Bessemer, Tuscaloosa, and Birmingham.

My parents continued to teach into the early 1930s while growing the business at the same time. My brother, Loren, was born in 1928 and I came along later in 1933. As the years passed and the business grew, my parents constructed more greenhouses and continued in the wholesale side into the late 1930s. At this time they decided to open a retail florist shop in our main building at the greenhouses in Bessemer. They continued in both wholesale and retail florist business through the thirties, forties, and the early fifties.

In the early 1950s, my father decided we would try to move to a new market because by then we had changed our business from selling mainly cut flowers to

Penny McHenry Hydrangea at Aldridge Gardens.

flowering potted plants and to foliage plants. Perhaps the most significant change—a moment of destiny—occurred in my family's life in 1951. That year my father located an empty building for rent at 322 South 20th Street in Birmingham. He moved the business into this new location and renamed it Aldridge Wholesale Floral Company from the original name of Bessemer Floral Company.

One day in early 1953, we were all returning to our greenhouses in Bessemer when we noticed a man putting a "For Sale" sign on the corner of Montgomery Highway and 21st Avenue South. His name was Dr. Bradley Waldron. We turned around to stop and ask him about the property, hoping we might find a permanent

Aldridge Garden Shop across from Vulcan Park.

location for our business. He named his price, and even though we thought it very high, we continued to talk about it on our trip back to Bessemer. The next day my father contacted Dr. Waldron only to learn that the price Dr. Waldron had quoted the previous day would be considerably higher because State Farm Insurance Company had just announced that they were going to build across the street. Even though we were stunned by the price increase, we agreed to buy the property from Dr. Waldron.

Our next big step was getting the land rezoned from residential to commercial. This began a battle with the residents on 21st Avenue. They had already succeeded in blocking an attempt to rezone land across the street from our location.

Snowflake Hydrangea Blossoms

George Taber Azalea.

Mr. Grayson of Grayson Lumber Company wanted to build a first-class motel there; after he lost his fight, he built unfinished shotgun houses on the property. These came to be known as the Grayson "spite" houses and remained on the property for many years.

We took our request for rezoning to Birmingham's commission form of city government. The residents on 21st Avenue hired an attorney to represent them and we hired our own. What ensued was a big fight in a crowded room at City Hall. Their lawyer accused us of wanting to rezone the land so we could sell the property to a liquor store. Our lawyer just listened to this and said nothing. My father, who had attended college with their lawyer, got up and told the opposing lawyer and the crowd that he had attended Alabama Polytechnic Institute with him and told him that he had no reason to attack his integrity. My father asked their attorney if he had ever known him to drink alcohol. Their lawyer said no. My father asked, do you really think I would sell to a liquor store. There was no response. The commission voted 2 to 1 to rezone the property commercial.

As it turned out, the decision by State Farm Insurance to build across the street that same year, 1953, worked in our favor—another moment of destiny. The corner lot we bought had a deep drop-off with only treetops showing from the road. State Farm had to remove a vast amount of soil to make room for their new building and we needed infill. The contractor came to us and offered us thousands of cubic yards of soil to fill in our property. We could not have built the quality building we did without this soil. Because of this wonderful location in the middle of a great gardening community, our business would be successful for over forty years.

A Family Business Through Good and Bad Times

I was allowed to leave high school in 1951, a half-year early, and enrolled in Auburn University following my brother, Loren, who had already graduated from Auburn in ornamental horticulture. Meanwhile my brother had begun to work at our Bessemer greenhouses after serving in the U.S. Army. His Army service had been cut short because of a medical condition that caused him to suffer continuous headaches.

Our parents took him to many doctors in search of an accurate diagnosis, and, finally, in May of 1952, my brother underwent surgery for a suspected problem in the optic nerve area; he died during the operation. The doctors had discovered a brain tumor that they suspected dated back to when he was nine years old.

Eddie Aldridge in Germany

My cousin, John McTyeire, was sent to Auburn to bring me home. Like my parents, I was completely devastated, and when I returned to school my concentration was gone and I became a student who just barely got by. When I asked my father what he thought about me joining the Army, he surprised me by agreeing that this would probably be best for me in the long run. In 1952, I did just that and served for two years, including postings at Fort Jackson, South Carolina; Fort Gordon, Georgia; Fort Lewis in Washington State; Fort Ord, California; and a full year in Germany. I was discharged in 1954 and began working for my parents at our first location on 20th street in Birmingham. When we bought the property at 21st Avenue, I helped clear the land.

Eddie and Mr. and Mrs. Aldridge in the mid seventies.

Two early employees, Beaty Hanna and Dick Black, were very important to the beginning of our business. After my brother's death in 1952, one of his classmates at Auburn, Beaty Hanna, started working at our Bessemer greenhouses and later moved to our new Birmingham location. He, along with another classmate, Dick Black, worked on adding more and more nursery items to our inventory and helped the business evolve into a full-scale nursery operation by late 1954. After my discharge from the Army, I worked in the nursery with Beaty and Dick in retail sales. Dick spent most of his time planting for our customers. Once I took over more of the business myself, Beaty and Dick were able to move on to successful landscape careers of their own. I managed the nursery from 1956 until my father died in 1978.

One of the biggest breaks in our family's struggling business came when my father negotiated with Channel Six television to trade out landscaping and maintenance services for advertising for our business. Channel Six broadcast our advertisements for many years, and this had a profound effect on our business in the entire Birmingham area as well as outlying communities in Jefferson and other counties. Our agreement with the channel lasted from the late fifties into the early seventies until there was a management change at the station.

Sometime after I had begun immersing myself in the family business, my father, who started his career as a science teacher, urged me to go back to school and finish my college training. He suggested I attend Birmingham-Southern College, both because of its excellent academic rating and because of its location. I was living with my parents in Bessemer at the time, and this would allow me to attend classes in the mornings and be at work at our nursery by noon. While this changed my course of study from the ornamental horticulture I had begun at Auburn to a liberal arts curriculum at Birmingham-Southern, I never regretted it. My studies included business and psychology as well as a minor in Latin, which proved very beneficial to me in my career. I worked hard and was a Dean's List student almost every quarter and was particularly proud of the fact that the G.I. Bill paid for my education.

While both Auburn and Birmingham-Southern helped shape my career, I had the best horticulture teacher one could hope for in my father, who taught me for twenty years. I worked by his side at our Birmingham nursery from 1955 until his death in 1978. At that time I moved on to manage our greenhouses in Bessemer while still helping manage the nursery. Through it all, I continued to

study and read everything possible about plants, and I am still learning today.

In recalling the progress of my family's business, I must pay tribute to the special role my mother played in its success. She worked upstairs at our Birmingham garden shop from 1954 to 1985. Added to the years she spent in our Bessemer greenhouses, she worked in our business for a total of sixty-two years without ever taking a salary. Although her father was a successful dentist in Bessemer and later a two-term mayor of Bessemer in the 1920s and early 1930s, she worked throughout her life out of pure dedication to my father and to our family business.

Setting My Sights on a New Property

In 1966, Mrs. John Coxe, who owned a home and twenty-seven acres on Rocky Ridge Ranch Road in Hoover, Alabama, came into our nursery and purchased two magnolia trees. She asked me to come out to her home and plant them. After I planted the trees, I went back to our nursery and told everyone I had seen a really beautiful piece of property situated on a lake. At that time, Hoover seemed

like a long way from eight miles. I had known Floyd Wallace, for a would come often into plants and fertilizer for next decade I must have my visit to Mrs. Coxe's The sequence of events made me firmly believe Gardens was destined to

In February of of men from our nursery nursery stock at our I stopped for fuel in trip to the farm and ran

Mr. John Coxe.

Mrs. Lyl Coxe.

Birmingham—about Mrs. Coxe's yardman, long time because he our nursery to purchase her property. Over the kept the memory of property firmly in mind. that eventually occurred that Aldridge Botanical happen.

1978, I was taking a crew in Birmingham to dig farm in Boaz, Alabama. English village for the into Floyd Wallace at the

Boathouse and geese on the lake.

Floyd Wallace stocking the lake about 1965.

service station. We greeted each other, and I asked him how everything was going at the Coxe home. He said everything was going well, except for the fact that Mrs. Coxe was going to sell the home and surrounding property. After this encounter, all I could think about on the way to the farm was how in the world I could afford a place like that.

About a year previous to 1978, I had sold my home on Shades Crest Road in Birmingham, and my accountant, Raymond Potter, kept reminding me that I needed to invest in another home to avoid paying capital gains on my previous home. With about $100,000 in savings, I knew that this home and property would be much more expensive than I could afford. When I returned from the farm that night, I called my father to ask his advice about the property, and he told me to call Mrs. Coxe and arrange a time for us to look at the home and grounds. The following Saturday, we

Old Photos
of the
Coxe Home

drove out for a visit. The first thing we noticed when we arrived was hundreds of survey stakes covering the grounds. After greeting Mrs. Coxe, the first thing I asked was what the wooden stakes meant. My heart sank when she told us the property was likely sold to a developer to build apartments, but the sale had not yet closed. I thought, oh well, I probably could not afford the property anyway.

Mrs. Coxe gave us a tour of her home, the home that would one day be an important part of Aldridge Botanical Gardens. Designed in 1964 by renowned Birmingham architect Henry Sprott Long, the home with its comfortable proportions and large open spaces seemed perfectly sited on its hillside overlooking the lake. Previous to the Coxe's building their home in the 1960's, Mrs. Coxe told me there was an older home built on the same site that was there for many years. The land was farmed. In fact, on the north side of the property, there are many terraces that were developed over the years. A portion of the property was used to grow various crops. These terraces are coming in handy for landscaping the north side of the property. A natural Alabama forest developed on this once farmed land and now provides the shade needed for our shade garden. Unfortunately John Coxe was killed by a runaway truck in Hoover a few years after the home was built. Mrs. Coxe had been living in the home for about twelve years with her maid and housekeeper.

Mrs. Coxe was reluctant to discuss any kind of price for the property. She told us that if the sale to the developer did not go through, we would have to discuss price with her daughter-in-law, Sahra Coxe, who was a realtor in Mountain Brook.

I knew that I wanted to buy this property. Just outside of Mrs. Coxe's front door, my father told me that if the property became available and if it did not cost more than a million dollars, I should buy it because it could be developed into a public garden someday. I was already discouraged about that beautiful place being bulldozed for apartments and went back to work disappointed about the possibility. At that time I did not contact Sahra Coxe because I felt sure the apartments were a certainty.

At this very moment, however, circumstances turned in our favor—another moment of destiny. Recently the Cahaba River Society had brought a lawsuit against Jefferson County for discharging sewage into the Cahaba River; overdevelopment was rampant, and the county had insufficient sewage

treatment plants. The very next week headlines in the newspaper read, "Jefferson County declares Sewage Moratorium on New Construction in South Jefferson County." That was the end of the plan for apartment development on my coveted property.

I couldn't believe this was really happening. I quickly made an appointment to meet with Sahra and Mrs. Coxe to talk about a possible purchase. I had the $100,000 and was hoping this would be enough for a down payment. When Sahra

The property in 1982.

quoted me a price, however, I felt that the property was still beyond my reach. I told Mrs. Coxe that it was scary for me to borrow that much money because I was in a very seasonal nursery business and some years were not as good as others. After telling her I was skeptical about paying off such a big loan, Mrs. Coxe offered to finance the property herself. She said that if I had a bad year in the business I could skip a year on the payment. Hardly believing my good fortune, I responded, "Mrs. Coxe, I want to buy this property." She sat down with tears in her eyes and said she was very happy because, she said, "You'll do the right thing."

Sentimental reasons aside, and notions of developing a public garden aside, I think the real reason I bought the property was simply because of my need to buy a new home and escape paying capital gains taxes. It had been well over a year since I sold my home on Shades Crest Road and Raymond Potter, our accountant, kept reminding me that I was running out of time to purchase another property. Of course I had studied enough economics in college to know that it was senseless to go several hundred thousand dollars in debt to save what would have been only a few thousand dollars in capital gains taxes from the previous home. Maybe it was correct for me to question my sanity…or maybe I was just following my inescapable destiny.

Raymond Potter, my accountant, was a World War II veteran and a very serious man who always had an unlit cigar in his mouth. When I called to tell him I had initially purchased a home before the deadline for capital gains taxes, he said he was relieved and hoped I had paid at least the same value as the house I had sold. When I told him I had paid about seven times more than I had paid for my first house, there was total silence on the other end of the phone. After he recovered, I explained, "But Mr. Potter, I got a better house and twenty-seven acres with a lake in the center of Hoover." He asked me how in the world I was going to pay for it. I explained that Mrs. Coxe had agreed to hold the mortgage and that she promised me I could skip a year of payment if I had a bad year in the business. Also, I explained how if it hadn't been for the moratorium on development in Hoover, I would have had to pay a lot more for the property. Somehow that did not make him feel any better. Time, of course, has proven that my decision—a seemingly extravagant one at the time—proved to be a wise one.

Personal Trials and Another Triumph

In the mid-seventies, a few years before my purchase of Mrs. Coxe's property, I was diagnosed with systemic lupus, a condition that really knocked me down. At the time I was living in a small concrete block house next to our garden shop and

Statue of St. Francis in the garden.

nursery. For almost a year I was crippled and confined to a chair in my little house. Our trusted employee Gordon Carlisle, a retired Marine, looked in on me constantly until I started my slow recovery.

In the fall of 1978, not long after my purchase of the Hoover property, my father died. At the time, I was working full time at the nursery while my mother was managing the upstairs garden shop. My father had been manager of our Bessemer greenhouses, and his death changed my life dramatically. I had to leave the nursery to take over the greenhouse operations full time, while still struggling to overcome the lupus. These traumatic events—the struggle with lupus, the loss of my father, having to quickly learn another part of our business, and managing the nursery long-distance—really took their toll on me.

I would leave my new home in Hoover at daylight every morning to work in the greenhouses in Bessemer and sometimes in the middle of the day would travel to Birmingham to manage the nursery for part of that day. Often, when driving home from such long days of work, I would question why I had ever bought the distant property in Hoover. I began to think about what my father had said in February of 1978 about someday developing the property into a public garden. Another turn in that direction was soon to come.

I remember Mrs. Coxe telling me that she and her husband had bought the twenty-seven acres from a Mr. Wilson and that he still owned the adjacent 3.2 acres

on the corner of Lorna Road and Rocky Ridge Ranch Road. Wilson had signed a covenant with the Coxes, agreeing not to sell the corner property for commercial development as long as the Coxe property remained residential. Mrs. Coxe told me that Wilson came to resent the covenant and would not agree to sell them the lot.

When I thought about the future possibility of developing a public garden, I knew I would have to buy Wilson's lot and tie it together with my own property.

The covenant with Wilson had transferred to me and while I did not know him, I thought he might be resentful to me for wanting to buy the corner land. In the spring of 1979, I hired an independent realtor to try to buy the property. He eventually succeeded and, for a hefty price, transferred the land to me. At the closing

Photos of
Corner Lot
on Lorna
Road

of the sale, I met Mr. and Mrs. Wilson in Mountain Brook and found them to be very nice people; they seemed to be glad to sell the property because of the covenant.

The corner lot on Rocky Ridge Ranch Road was a very large open ditch with large boulders about eight to ten feet below road level covering almost an acre of my new property. It was hard to imagine what I could do with this unsightly lot. At this point in time, in the spring of 1979, I found myself in deep debt. I had probably paid too much for the Wilson land and now had extremely high payments to make on both properties. I began to consider my sanity on subjecting myself to so much debt and additional stress while trying to fight a debilitating disease. I still wonder today how I managed to survive the lupus, keep running the business, and make the necessary payments to the bank. My dream of someday fulfilling my father's suggestion to create a public garden must have bolstered my determination. I think I was moving towards a goal that was much greater than myself.

I became aware that Harbert Construction was contracted to widen Lorna Road to four lanes from Highway 31 in Vestavia to the part of Highway 31 where the proposed Galleria mall would be built. I contacted John Harbert and asked him if there was a possibility of getting several thousand cubic yards of soil, which I knew he would be displacing, to fill in the mini-canyon on my corner lot. He said that not only was it possible, it would save him a great deal to haul the soil to our location, which was only three to four hundred yards from the part of Lorna Road he had to lower by several feet. He was so excited about this possibility that he offered not only to move the soil into my lot but also to compact it with his equipment and create a forty-foot entrance to the corner property when he poured the curbs.

Mr. Harbert also offered me some valuable advice. He told me we needed to install a large drainage pipe to drain the property to the county storm sewer before they filled in the lot. He also told me that since I had no sewer line on the property,

Walkways on the corner lot installed by the city of Hoover.

I should stub a main line across Lorna Road to the trunk line before they paved the road. He said that this line should be large enough to accommodate whatever future development I planned for the property. I hired Walter Schoel Engineering and they designed two drainpipes and the sewer line across Lorna Road. We ended up with a large concrete pipe running north south on Lorna Road and also east west to the

storm sewer, thus completely draining the corner property. Harbert Construction installed the pipes and sewer line then quickly followed with the soil, compacting and pouring of the entrance curb.

The cost of the engineering and installation, between $25,000 and $30,000, added yet more to my debt, but there was a 100 percent improvement to the property; not only was the drainage provided for, but the entire thirty acres looked much better. This was the second time in my life that I was given many thousands of cubic yards of soil for free. Looking at the 3.2-acre corner property today, I'm not sure it was not the best purchase I made of the now thirty acres. As far as the gardens are concerned, without that acreage on Lorna Road, there would not have been many possibilities. We would not have the main entrance on Lorna Road, the beautiful stone wall across the front with the signage would not have been possible, nor would there have been room for our first 100 parking places. The paved walkways that wind throughout the corner property with its bridge installed by the city of Hoover would not have been there. The openness at the main entrance to the gardens would not have been achieved. The landscaping possibilities would have been limited. The wooded areas on the corner property would likely have been destroyed by future commercial development. And finally, the gardens would not have been awarded Beautification Awards from both the city of Hoover and the Jefferson County Beautification Boards. Looking back today, that purchase, one year after the purchase of the home with its twenty-seven acres proved to be an extremely important part of the over-all garden.

Another step toward a garden of destiny was achieved. All that was left was the huge debt that I would continue to pay for the next ten years. The only bright spot in my financial picture during this period was that the interest payments on my debt were so great that they reduced my yearly income taxes to very little. For this I was grateful.

We Build a Nest…and So Do the Hornets

Our business continued to do well through the late seventies and eighties, and so I was able to take enough salary to make those payments on both of my Hoover properties. While work was going well, my personal life may have been lagging. On June 12 of 1981, friends brought this wonderful person named Kay

Eddie and Kay.

Shackelford Rockett out to my home for dinner and my life changed dramatically. My health began to steadily improve and life seemed worthwhile once again. Kay and I married on October 17, 1981, in the great room of my Hoover home. Along with

Kay, I had the good fortune to gain a fourteen-year-old young man named Jimmy Rockett, a dog named Bambi, and a cat named Jeremiah. To this day we remain totally connected and headed down the same path.

When I first met Kay, we would walk around the grounds and talk about my father's vision for the property to one day become a public garden. She never questioned my dream to fulfill this vision. I had been questioning my sanity since purchasing the properties in 1978 and 1979, but now, with Kay's support, I felt that the entire venture was beginning to make sense.

After we married, I decided to lease the nursery part of our operation, and that relieved the strain of having too much to manage. My mother continued to work and manage the garden center until her mid-eighties, and then Kay took over her job, managing with excellence until we closed the business in 1995.

Kay and I settled into the Hoover home and over the next eighteen years we would have many adventures with the land and with what lived and grew on it. One of our earliest and most memorable experiences was what we came to call the martin house/hornets' nest event. Before I bought the Hoover property, the Coxe family had installed two martin houses next to the lake. One was between the two

Waterfall we installed on the property with first basketball goal in background.

magnolias that I had once planted for Mrs. Coxe, and it was now consumed by the ever-growing trees; the other was on the opposite side of the house by the cove next to the lake. The martin houses were elaborate wooden structures with several rooms; both were mounted on top of telephone poles. When they were about twenty years old, the houses began to rot and no longer attracted martins. After a few years, we started to notice what we thought were bees flying out of the martin house on the cove. We didn't pay much attention to this until we noticed hornet-type nesting bulging outside of the house. We soon discovered that these really were hornets, as we watched them come and go.

I had heard all my life the expression "as mean as a hornet." One day when cutting the grass, I learned what that expression really meant. As I was riding the mower, I had my eye focused on the hornet-infested martin house and actually watched as a hornet left the nest and made a "beeline" straight to my right knee. I felt an incredibly sharp pain. Now I became obsessed with getting rid of the nest. I first tried spraying a hornet and wasp killer from a small ladder, but the nest was so high and so massive that the spray would not quite reach or penetrate the nest. Next I had the bright idea of using a small dump truck that I kept on the property to knock the nest down. Letting the tailgate down to the flat position, I backed into the pole holding the nest, and, as I hit the pole, the martin house and hornets' nest went plunging into the lake. I had the windows closed tightly, and with no air-conditioning in the truck, I still remember the summer heat broiling me. As I ran for my life to the front door of the house, I could see hundreds of hornets swarming around the floating martin house in the lake. The house continued to float for weeks, and we didn't venture out until it disappeared in the lake. We knew we'd made those "mad" hornets even madder…and we didn't want to take any more chances.

One of the many Southern Magnolias on the property.

Our Own Little Golf Course

Sometime after Kay and I married, I developed an interest in golf. After so many years of constant work, we decided to take off at least a half-day a week and try our hand at the game. We started playing at Oak Mountain State Park and later on the course at Oxmoor Valley. However, in the nursery business in the South, the busy season is most of

Kay in the golf cart by the lake.

the year, and so we found ourselves with less and less time to go to a golf course. The solution: why not create a small course in the space available around our home and lake. So began our adventure with a home golf course.

I decided to build our own nine-hole chipping and putting course, making a circle around the house. The greens were about fifteen feet across and spaced from sixty to ninety feet apart. I hauled in lots of topsoil for the greens and raised them about twelve inches above the ground level. I planted them with bent grass and installed cups and flags. We really enjoyed practicing on our little course, but before long I realized just how much maintenance

Bridge donated by Henry and Shannon Long and dedicated to their children Henry III, Mark and Hope.

was required on the greens, such as mowing every third day. After about two years, and some deliberation, I decided to remove the course. At least we enjoyed playing at home for that short period, and over the years our little golf course has been the source of a lot of interesting conversation.

What We Learned about Goats

*W*hen I first bought the property in 1978, I realized by mid-summer that invasive plants—especially Chinese privet— seemed to be taking over the woodlands surrounding the house. Since all of the original twenty-seven acres had a fence, I had the bright idea of purchasing a pair of goats. Horace Washington, an employee at the garden shop who had become a friend and who spent a lot of time with me at the new house, helped locate a pair of goats in Locust Fork. We headed that way to pick them up. When we arrived, we managed to load the nanny goat on the truck but had to pull the billy goat by his horns. As we were loading him, Horace had turned his back on the billy goat and the goat butted him in the rear up against the cab of

the truck. After more struggling, we finally tied the goats securely in the back of the truck. As we drove back to Hoover, I had wonderful visions of these goats eating all of that Chinese privet.

When we unloaded the pair, they took off immediately to explore their new territory. When I first bought the property, I had planted several Japanese maples that my father had grown from seed. They had leafed out that spring and were really pretty. Well, guess what the goats decided to eat. It was not the Chinese privet. In

1923 Ford Touring Car.

spite of this unexpected behavior, I remained optimistic about our goats. Though I had gotten off to a bad start with my newly acquired stock, I just knew they would eventually settle into eating the Chinese privet.

During the 1970s, I had purchased a 1923 Ford touring car and had it completely refurbished, including a new cloth top. The car was in my open garage. When I returned home from work the next day, the goats were standing in my Model T and had eaten almost the entire top. The goats remained on the property for another week, and as far as I can remember, they never did eat any Chinese privet. They jumped the fence and escaped into the unknown. So much for my brilliant idea about goats.

The Case of the Attacking Swans

Horace and I decided that what the lake really needed was a pair of mute swans. We had heard about a man—again in Locust Fork—who raised swans and other birds. So off we went, this time returning with a pair of white swans. Our lives would never be the same. The swans were beautiful floating on the lake, and I enjoyed feeding them with cracked corn under the redwood (Metasequoia) tree. We didn't know at the time that the swans would take total possession, not only of the lake, but also of the entire thirty-acre property.

The pair produced quite a few cygnets every year, but we had a real problem with hawks plucking the young ones from the water. They were totally defenseless against the hawks. Just before Kay and I married, someone threw a firecracker into the lake and one of the swans picked it up; it blew his throat out and he eventually died. We purchased another male and later he mated with our female and she had more cygnets. I had been told that when the same swans mated they did so for life. So much for that theory.

The white swans were so beautiful that I decided to go back to Locust Fork and purchase a pair of black ones. These black swans were

Swans
on the Lake

natives of Australia and still did their mating on Australian time or in the middle of our winter. Because the two pairs of swans had different mating seasons, there was a constant war between them. And their battle eventually extended to us. We had purchased a small boat with a six-horse motor and occasionally would ride around the lake in the late afternoon. The swans seemed to be offended by our presence and would fly into the side of the boat, flapping their wings as hard as they could against the boat. When we tried to swim in the lake, the swans attacked us and we had to exit the water as soon as possible.

Over the years, we let many groups use our property, including Audubon, scouts, church groups, and others. On one occasion a scout troop was having a canoe demonstration on the edge of the lake. The group was led by Everett Holle, a local television personality. I warned Everett that the black swans were very aggressive and might try to disrupt the canoe demonstration, but he told me he thought the instructor could handle any situation. At one point I looked to the far side of the lake and saw the male black swan swimming very fast toward the canoe demonstration and the audience of scouts gathered on the bank of the lake. I knew trouble was on the way. When the swan approached the canoe, he lunged out of the water and hit the instructor in the middle of his body. The instructor hit the water headfirst, while the swan continued to flap his wings and lunge at him. The scouts rescued their instructor and that was the end of canoe demonstration for the day.

We also allowed some fishermen to fish in the lake, but of course the swans did not like this either. One day we came home from work and saw the male black swan limping. On closer observation, we saw a large hook was lodged in his foot.

Our guess was that a fisherman

then cut the fishing line loose.

in capturing the swan and wrestling

drove as I held onto the swan in

arrived at the vet's office, I took a

wings. When you grab a swan this

and their legs straight back, very

entered the office, which was full

you can't imagine the disruption

simply sprayed the swan's foot with

and removed the prickly hooks.

another disruption as we exited

the lake with our recovering

One January, our

nest next to the boathouse.

morning when I decided

to check on the eggs.

beginning to hatch and

the nest. The male black

same time I saw him,

and half-flying toward

with me because I

especially aggressive

had hooked the curious swan and

Horace Washington and I succeeded

him into my station wagon. Horace

the back with all my might. When we

firm hold on the muscle of the swan's

way, they stretch their necks out straight

much like they are in full flight. As we

of ladies with their pets in their laps,

we caused. Dr. Price, the veterinarian,

WD-40, cut the barb with a wire cutter,

The operation completed, we created

the office. We went straight back to

swan.

Australian black swan was on the

It was a very cold and frosty

to go down the small bank

When I arrived, the eggs were

one cygnet was already in

swan saw me about the

and he started swimming

me. I had carried a broom

knew the swans were

when they were nesting.

I started running up the bank towards the house, but my feet slipped on the frosty ground and down I came. The swan jumped on me and started flogging me with his powerful wings. I finally got up and started swinging the broom at the swan. He kept after me all the way to the sun porch. Kay witnessed this beating, and I pleaded with her not to tell anybody that I had been totally whipped by a black swan. The temperature that morning was zero degrees, and I still remember the cold ground. We named the first cygnet that hatched Zero because of the weather that day.

One day when Kay was jogging in the driveway, the black swans flew into her from the woods and knocked her down. This was the beginning of the end for all the swans. We decided to return all four back to the farm in Locust Fork. The next day, after the usual feeding of cracked corn, I threw a sheet over the swans, one by one, and carried them to the van for the drive back to their original home. The era of the swans was over. Although they had been with us for more than eighteen years, we never succeeded in developing a positive relationship with them.

One final swan tale: I built a chipping area on the side of the lake opposite from the house. I would often chip golf balls across the lake to one of the greens in the front yard. The swans had a habit of standing on the edge of the bank on one foot and sleeping. One day as I was chipping balls across the lake, one of the balls came down directly behind the swan's neck and completely knocked him out. As I quickly ran to the swan, expecting the worse, he slowly but surely stood up with a dazed look. I was relieved. In my short golf career, this was my only "birdie."

Our Woodland Fitness Center

In 1982, I decided to install a basketball goal outside by the garage, along with lighting so that I could exercise at night. It seemed that I suffered less from the lupus when I exercised, and so I was determined to do as much as possible. I used the new goal almost every night and my health steadily improved. Even in wintertime

I would put on a coat and hat and gloves and go out to shoot some baskets. I was a far cry from being good at basketball, and the additional clothing did little to help my performance. After one cold night outside, I told Kay that we should consider building a gymnasium up in the woods where we could both exercise together at night after work. That was fine with her, and so we contracted with a company to build our gym. The result was a forty-by sixty-foot building with a nineteen-foot ceiling. The building was constructed for year-round use with large fans on one end, windows that could be raised across the other end, and a gas heater. We also installed large windows on both sides so we could enjoy views of the surrounding woodland. I had my basketball goal, Kay had her treadmill, and we even had a complete badminton court. A pool table and TV added to our exercise and entertainment. We ended up using the gym almost every night and enjoyed it immensely. This marked the beginning of a lifetime of exercise, a habit that we continue today in the gym beneath our new home. Kay and I agree that both of our gyms are one reason that we are still around.

Clearing for Azaleas and Hydrangeas

In the 1980s, we began a major cleanup of the woodlands on both sides of our driveway, a project that began to give space and shape to our property. We thinned out all of the small trees and underbrush, leaving all the larger ones. The pines now had room to develop full heads and we gained a lot of useful space. I decided that this newly cleared area would be good for the winter storage of azaleas. During those years we sold a lot of azaleas from Mobile, where they would bloom very early. We began bringing most of the azalea plants from our nursery to our home property in the fall, letting them lie dormant in winter until the appropriate blooming time for our

Hydrangea Paniculata Grandiflora 'Tardiva'.

area. Then they would be transported to our garden shop for spring sales. We did this for several years and it worked well, though it did involve a lot of labor. Eventually we quit transporting the azaleas to our property and began bringing them directly to our nursery while they were still dormant in winter. Our efforts were not wasted, however. We ended up with a lot of cleared woodland space, better growth on our

Camellia Sasanqua.

large trees, and lots of room to plant hydrangeas, especially the 'Snowflake' and 'Harmony' hydrangeas that our family discovered, propagated, and, in the case of 'Snowflake', eventually patented.

These hydrangeas are such an important part of our family history and Aldridge Gardens, that a little background is in order. Most hydrangeas have their origins in Asia and the United States, and our two native species are found mostly in the Southeast. They were discovered in the 1700s by botanists John and William Bartram and were called Hydrangea arborescens or smooth hydrangea and Hydrangea quercifolia or oakleaf hydrangea. The 'Snowflake' and 'Harmony' varieties that my family discovered were developed from chance seedlings of Hydrangea quercifolia.

While the hydrangea is Aldridge Garden's signature plant, the planting of many Camellias through the years has brightened the gardens during the fall and winter months. We consider it our signature plant for that time of year.

Success of the Camellia plantings has resulted in Aldridge Gardens being named as part of the National American Camellia Society Trails across the United States.

The Camellia was chosen for additional plantings because it is Alabama's official State Flower.

Camellia.   Snow Queen Oak Leaf Hydrangea.   Indica Azalea.

The Story of 'Snowflake'

My father, Loren L. Aldridge, was well into his horticultural business in June of 1969 when a neighbor brought him a bloom from a hydrangea that he had never seen before. My father asked the neighbor to take us to the plant, which he had discovered in a lady's backyard in Lipscomb, Alabama. We found the plant to be in not very good condition. The owner allowed us to take three cuttings from the plant, and we carried them to our greenhouse to be propagated. All three of the cuttings rooted, and we transplanted them to four-inch pots. When they reached about six inches tall in the fall, we took the plants to our display area at our garden center in Birmingham. All three

Mr. Loren Aldridge with Snowflake Hydrangea in 1975.

Snowflake
Hydrangeas

plants leafed out, showing they were off to a good start. I was very proud of these plants, and I watched them closely.

That spring I assigned one of our employees to pull weeds while I was out planting trees. When I returned from the planting, I quickly discovered that the hydrangeas had been pulled and tossed into the dumpster. I sent this employee

Kay standing next to a Snowflake Hydrangea planting at Aldridge Gardens.

headfirst into the dumpster to retrieve the cuttings. The plants were severely damaged but we repotted all three, two of which quickly died. The original plant in Lipscomb had also died, so we were down to a single cutting. This one managed to survive, however, and the next year we made another cutting from the plant, followed by several more cuttings over the next three years. Once we reached thirteen cuttings, we knew we had enough to begin serious cultivation of the plant. We planted those

Snowflake in early June with its multiple emerging sepals.

Hydrangea Quercifolia Snowflake afer 8 weeks in bloom.

original thirteen hydrangeas next to the waterfall in the garden. They still stand there today, as beautiful as ever.

Once I realized this plant would have a great future, I decided in 1970 to apply for a U.S. plant patent. Over the years we had sold many different patented plants and had observed how these plants got a lot of publicity. Before we had rooted 100 of our hydrangeas, it had already appeared in several magazines. At that time there was only one law firm in Chicago that specialized in plant patents, and so we applied to them. When we received the patent in 1971, the plant was immediately publicized in several horticulture magazines. We didn't know enough about patents at that time to know that we could have charged royalties on our cuttings. It took years to have enough cuttings for our own use. Our only reason for wanting a patent was the publicity. We never charged a royalty on the plant. And publicity we did get;

in fact, the publicity got way ahead of our production. Throughout the 1970s we had very few to sell at our nursery. During those years we carried most of the rooted cuttings to our farm in Boaz, Alabama, and lined them out for future cuttings. Most of those plants are still on our farm today.

Just what makes Snowflake so different from the native species? The native species has both fertile flowers and sterile flowers or sepals. The fertile flowers, followed by seed, form alongside the stem of the panicle, and the sterile flowers (sepals) occur on the tips of the florets. There are usually four sepals. The 'Snowflake'

Eddie with Snowflake Hydrangea in the late flowering stage.

hydrangea forms multiple sepals on the floret with no seed. The sepals (flowers in sets of four) open in sequence over several weeks and the entire panicle has multiple

Emerging sepals on Snowflake Hydrangea.

double flowers. As the panicle matures, the back sepals on the floret turn pink as new sepals keep emerging. At this stage the panicle is spectacular and its beauty lasts about eight weeks. Because 'Snowflake' has only sterile sepals with no seed, the plant must be propagated from cuttings. We patiently carried out this kind of propagation for many years. A new type of propagation from tissue culture has emerged in recent years; this method takes small bits of leaf tissue with the proper amount of DNA and starts their growth in test tube-type cylinders. This has speeded up the process and increased the number of plants available worldwide.

During the 1980s and 90s, we were propagating enough 'Snowflake' hydrangeas from our farm to have about 200 plants a year for sale at our garden center. They sold for the grand price of $5.95 each, and we probably sold two or three thousand to the public during those years. The market price today is, of course, considerably higher. A nursery friend told us he had spotted a plant in a six-inch pot with one bloom in Japan selling for $300.

Our 'Snowflake' hydrangea quickly found its way around the country and the world. We gave away many to botanical gardens across the country, with the largest amount going to the Birmingham Botanical Gardens, Callaway Gardens in Pine Mountain, GA. and to gardens in the Northeast and Northwest. In the 1980s, the Garden Club of America met in Birmingham, and we gave every member a plant, thus increasing distribution across the United States. In 1980, we shipped about 200 plants to France, and from there they were sent to many European countries as well as Japan. The French company agreed to pay for the first plants, but after an agreement to share sales we received nothing for future sales.

A word about the naming of 'Snowflake': when I first applied for the patent, the name I suggested was Snowcap. When I was stationed in the Pacific Northwest during my Army years, I had a daily view of the snowcapped mountains and remained ever impressed. However, after more time observing the flower and arching effect of the blooms on our hydrangea, as well as the intricate make-up of the plant's emerging sepals, I thought the bloom truly resembled a magnified snowflake.

This change from 'Snowcap' to 'Snowflake' may have helped propel the plant to its popularity. We had discovered a southern way to have snowflakes in May, June, and July. The plant does of course grow in milder northern climates such as New England, the Northwest Coast, along with some locations in California, Europe, and Asia. I never dreamed the plant would become a favorite in Europe and Japan.

'Harmony'—Another Discovery

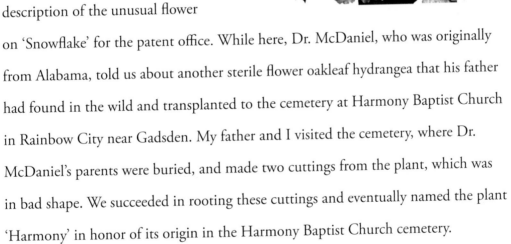

When we applied for the patent on 'Snowflake', we called Dr. J. C. McDaniel, a professor of horticulture from the University of Illinois and an expert on native hydrangeas. Dr. McDaniel came to Birmingham and wrote a description of the unusual flower on 'Snowflake' for the patent office. While here, Dr. McDaniel, who was originally from Alabama, told us about another sterile flower oakleaf hydrangea that his father had found in the wild and transplanted to the cemetery at Harmony Baptist Church in Rainbow City near Gadsden. My father and I visited the cemetery, where Dr. McDaniel's parents were buried, and made two cuttings from the plant, which was in bad shape. We succeeded in rooting these cuttings and eventually named the plant 'Harmony' in honor of its origin in the Harmony Baptist Church cemetery.

Although it is also a sterile flower hydrangea, 'Harmony' looks entirely different from 'Snowflake'. The blooming panicle is very large and entirely full of sepals that are very compact. The sepals do not open in sequence like 'Snowflake', but the bloom is likewise spectacular. Although 'Harmony" is also a great beauty, 'Snowflake' continued to outsell it about five or six to one. We decided not to apply for a patent on 'Harmony'.

Stormy Weather

Shortly after Kay and I married in 1982, we had a mid-winter blizzard in Birmingham that crippled the whole area for more than a week. A lot of snow was followed by extreme cold for three or four days. I remember taking a photo of the

Snowstorm of 1982.

thermometer next to the kitchen, and it registered minus one degree. We lost our power and remained stranded for six or seven days, forcing us to cook on the gas grill outside the house and keep warm

by huddling next to the fireplace in the great room. When all of our cut wood was burned up in two days, I roamed the property in the snow looking for dry wood.

Snowstorm of 1993.

After sleeping for days next to the fireplace, where we could only warm one side of us at a time, we made the decision to install a wood-burning stove on the sun porch.

Fortunately, this stove was installed and we had stored plenty of wood outside the sun porch when the next big storm hit on March 13, 1993. This was the worst storm I had ever seen, and I recall it being not just a snowstorm but a thunderstorm as well. I remember the loud blasts of pine trees breaking from the overload of snow, and we watched as the branches of our large cedars in the front yard also crashed to the ground. Every pine tree lining the driveway fell across the drive, blocking us in with no power for over a week. The entire thirty acres was left in a grand mess of fallen trees and limbs, and it would take us more than two years to clean up from this

storm. By the time we formed a trust with the city of Hoover in 1995 to establish Aldridge Gardens, we had most of the property cleaned up. I hired an arborist to trim and sculpture the big cedars, and today they are looking good again.

In Pursuit of a Dream

In the mid 1980s, the city of Hoover contacted us about selling the property to them. They wanted to relocate their city hall away from the busy intersection on Highway 31 and I-459 before they started building a recreation center in the same area. A delegation, including Mayor Frank Skinner and Alan Pate, director of operations, came over and talked to us about the plans. We thanked them but told them of our dream to somehow turn the property into a public garden. I explained that I was aware of the fact that the city could use their right of eminent domain to acquire the property. Mayor Skinner was quick to reply that the city had no intention of doing that. This meeting perhaps sowed a seed with the city officials that eventually led to their offer of a trust to form the gardens. In any case, Kay and I now started talking seriously about developing our thirty acres into a public garden.

In earlier years, we had actually made some moves in that direction. As part of our plan, we wanted to enlarge the lake and develop the high ground that ran between our home and the dam on the eastern edge of the property. The State Conservation Department helped us by drawing up plans to create a large island surrounded by water. However, as they were studying the impact of the plan, they determined that people living in an apartment complex just below the existing dam would be at risk. This, along with high legal costs, brought an end to our idea of developing a garden on our own. Our lawyer also told us he was uncertain how long it would take to form a private foundation. We had already invested a lot of money in the project, but with such a large acreage and the uncertainty of my health, we knew we could not stay there forever. In addition, we had a problem with strangers coming onto the property to fish in the lake and had no way to control this. We continued to talk about a public garden.

Farmers in the garden.

Our next move was to contact Auburn University to determine if they would accept a charitable trust to develop the property into a garden. My father had graduated from Auburn in 1926 and my brother in 1950. We negotiated for about a year but could never reach an agreement, mainly because Auburn had an interim president at the time. They understood that this was not a gift of land that could be sold and added to the endowment, but would have to be kept in perpetuity as a public garden.

Our third attempt was to approach the city of Hoover to see if they had any interest in helping us fulfill our dreams for the property. We met again with Mayor Frank Skinner, and he understood what our property could mean to the city. His answer was yes. From that point on we worked with Mayor Skinner and Alan Pate, his director of operations. They were the two people most responsible for carrying through with the trust and making the gardens become a reality. Alan came up with the terms of the trust long before it was finalized with a lawyer. The most important issue to us was our determination that the property be dedicated in

perpetuity as a garden. We had the property appraised twice; one appraiser did not include the lake as part of the property and another appraiser included the lake, home, and corner property. We went to Alan Pate with the figures we received and offered to subtract value from the appraisal if the city, by resolution, would dedicate the property in perpetuity. They agreed.

Learning about Trusts

*I*n the beginning, I knew very little about trusts. My father had once loaned my cousin, Arthur Aldridge, and his wife, Martha, money to build their new home in Boaz in 1970. They made payments to my parents, and after my father died, they continued payments to my mother. My mother and I decided to develop an education trust for their younger children with the mortgage. At the time, I thought my mother had sufficient funds for the rest of her life. However, she lived to be almost ninety and, as we chose to care for her in her own home, her savings were quickly depleted with sitters and other costs, up to $70,000 a year. Her funds ran very low, and I thought the trust had been a mistake. However, the trust did work as planned and paid for the education of my cousin's children.

Our second trust was to be with Hoover to fund the gardens. I consulted with officers at AmSouth (now Regions Bank), and they gave me a handout on all the different kinds of trusts. Alan Pate had already suggested that we use a CRUT, a charitable remainder unitrust, for the gardens. This pays a lifetime income that can fluctuate with the market. A third trust we set up was a personal one for our former business, which pays us income for life and will benefit the gardens at our death. I will never forget, however, that in setting up this trust, we had to pay a great deal of money in taxes up front because of increased values to our company.

We set up a fourth trust, another CRUT, to the Auburn University Department of Ornamental Horticulture to establish an Eminent Scholar Chair

Hydrangea Quercifolia Snowflake afer 6 weeks in bloom.

in memory of my brother. We use a lot of the income from the last three trusts for various charitable gifts, including $20,000 a year for an intern program at the gardens. We also give five to seven thousand dollars to other projects at the gardens every year, as well as other charities.

When we were on a garden tour of Wales and the Lake Country of England in 2006, we visited many public gardens sanctioned by the Royal Horticulture Society. Most of these gardens were protected by being in the National Trust, but none of the individual gardens were in any kind of trust. I asked our garden tour director what would eventually happen to their gardens. He said there was a saying among gardeners in Great Britain that the garden dies with the gardener. In the U.S. we have organizations such as the Garden Conservancy that attempt to preserve special private gardens. In our case, the charitable trust we set up and the dedication of the land by the city of Hoover assures that this garden will be preserved. We had an ironclad trust.

Building Our New Home

Once we were in negotiations with Hoover to begin the gardens, Kay and I knew we would have to think about moving. The city of Hoover would allow us to live in our current home for one year. It was time to look for a new site. Riding

Eddie, Missy and Kay.

around on a Sunday afternoon, we discovered a new subdivision called Highland Lakes in North Shelby County. We drove up and down the roads until I located a lake. After our years in Hoover, we knew we wanted another home on a lake. I spotted a beautiful lot with a small entrance that flared out next to the lake. The lot started out with a gentle slope, peaked in the middle, and then sloped to the water. My first question from Kay when I got back in the car was, "You're not going to move me way up here, are you?" I could just visualize building on that peak with a gym under the house. Once the trust with Hoover was settled, we bought this lot at Highland Lakes.

Our Hoover home was so livable that we decided to use the original Henry Sprott Long plans for our new home. We both loved the one-level living and general layout of the home. However, the width of the home was too great for the lot we had fallen in love with. Several weeks later, we bought a second lot adjacent to the one

New home with Fall colors.

Walter and Tommy.

we had chosen. Even before beginning the building, we had spent half the money Hoover paid us for our home and six acres. I knew then that we were going to be spending some real money. We found a builder and got started early in the summer of 1995.

We enjoyed many trips to our building site during the construction process, and we are happy to report that the home turned out just as we had hoped. When the home was completed in 1996, I began landscaping our new two acres. In fact, I did so much landscaping that we jokingly call our yard "Aldridge Gardens East." Walter Eakin, who started working in our greenhouses around 1950, and his son Tommy have been helping us with many projects at our new home over the last ten years. Both Walter and Tommy were also involved in getting our 'Snowflake' hydrangea and camellias established at our Hoover property. In fact, they have been invaluable to us on projects at both our home and the public gardens.

From Trust to Groundbreaking

*t*he year 1997 saw the real beginning of the gardens when the city of Hoover named several people as incorporators before a board was formed. Besides myself, these were Barbara Sims and Peggy Knight, along with Virginia Williams, director of development for the city. We worked together with city officials to choose an architectural firm for the project. After a number of interviews, we selected Environmental Planning and Design from Pittsburgh, Pennsylvania, to do the master

Bridge at the end of the dam installed by the city of Hoover in 2002.

plan for the garden. The principals of the design team notified the city that they would have to have a detailed topographical map of the property before drawing up the plan. Kay and I gave a donation to the Endowment Fund to pay for this map, which was done by Walter Schoel Engineering. Once completed, the architects started on the master plan, which was paid for by the city of Hoover.

After the master plan was completed, Mayor Skinner and the incorporators named members of the board. This original board consisted of Mayor Skinner, John Floyd, Jessie Bean, Louise Wrinkle, William Billingsley, Peggy Knight, Tina Kitchens, Barbara Sims, Bob Heald, Judy Funk, myself, and Virginia Williams ex-officio. During the following years, these board members would make great contributions toward the building of the gardens. Two of our original board members, John Floyd and Louise Wrinkle, had many years of experience with botanical gardens and brought much expertise to the beginning of our garden.

Before the master plan was completed, the city had the land rezoned agricultural and took the responsibility of building a new spillway on the dam and also a bridge over the spillway. Then in 2001, the city developed a $2-million challenge bond and promised to match dollar for dollar all contributions from individuals, corporations, and foundations. A capital campaign was then undertaken. Board members were asked to make pledges and everybody made a commitment. Kay and I made a pledge and later gave additional funds to build the cascade waterfall. Once the pledges started coming in and the city began matching these funds, the board and the city decided it was time to break ground for the new garden.

Beginning of Kay's Woodland Stream.

Frog pond donated by Gene and Pam Smith in memory of his mother, Elaine Baird Smith.

Our groundbreaking took place on September 15, 2001, a few days after the disaster of 9-11. We were afraid that this would be a bad time to run a capital fund-raising campaign for a garden. Board member Bob Heald suggested that we ask Tony Tanner to be our capital campaign chairman. Once he visited the home and grounds and viewed the master plan, he agreed to become chairman. In addition, he and his wife pledged a large gift in honor of their mothers, Martha Crabb and Cleo Tanner. This large gift kick-started the campaign and the money began coming in at a steady level, along with the matching funds.

A Garden Takes Shape

*J*efferson County provided a crew to do all the preliminary work for our new parking lot, including tree and stump removal, hauling in hundreds of yards of chert and gravel for our subpaving. This was a huge gift to the gardens. The city of Hoover also did many in-kind jobs, such as paving the parking lot and adding stone curbs.

Opening Day Ceremonies, June 1, 2002.

We had enough money to install all of our electrical lines underground all the way to the dam. All the poles and wires were removed, creating a great improvement in the property.

While all this work was going on outside, the city was having new bathrooms and a lot of plumbing work done in the house. One of the main projects was having

Kay's Woodland Stream.

sewage lines installed from the home out to main lines. The house would become a focal point for many events in the gardens and so these improvements were major ones.

Eddie and Kay on Opening Day, June 1, 2002.

With funds given by Tony and Elizabeth Tanner and some additional contributions, we were able to install a shade garden on the southeast side of the property. The plan for this garden, designed by local landscape architects Nimrod Long and Associates, included a water feature—a stream from the shade garden recirculating down to the lake. Board member John Floyd, editor of Southern Living magazine, felt strongly that we needed that stream installed before officially opening the gardens. Kay and I decided to make a donation to install the stream, and I asked the board to name it Kay's Woodland Stream. Our donation was a gift of stock—6,800 shares— that had a very high value, and we transferred the stock at that value. By the end of that week, the stock had fallen to a very low value. Was this destiny again? That gift paid for the woodland stream, which was completed in the winter of 2001.

In addition to the shade garden, we completed one mile of walking trails, including a half-mile trail around the lake funded by Southern Progress Corporation. We were almost ready for our opening. A committee selected Don Barber to be the director of our new gardens, and he selected Pat Scholund as his assistant. On a hot day in June of 2002, Aldridge Gardens were officially opened with about 5,000 people attending. It was a proud moment for me and Kay, for the city of Hoover, and for all those who had made so many contributions to this grand undertaking.

The new pavilion built in 2005.

The Garden Blooms and Grows

Ever since that opening day, development of the gardens has continued onward. From the very beginning the public responded to the gardens, both as a place of serenity in which to enjoy peaceful walks and as a beautiful venue for events such as weddings. A full schedule of corporate meetings, plant sales, symposiums, horticulture classes, and much more became the order of the day. To accommodate the growing list of events, the board decided in 2004 to build a pavilion where our home gym once existed. The new pavilion was completed in 2005, along with new restrooms and a catering kitchen next to the pavilion. CLA Architecture, Inc. of Birmingham volunteered to design the building as well as supervise its construction. Judy Funk, a founding board member, and her husband, David, of David Funk Engineering volunteered for all the engineering work.

There are a number

"Come along", donated by Mr. and Mrs. Bob Smith to honor their grandchildren, Michael, Drew, Mary Kate, Gracie, Abby and Emmy.

of major annual events in the gardens. Every June we have our largest event, a fund-raiser called "Hydrangeas under the Stars." Every spring and fall we feature a huge hydrangea sale, and those same seasons see a large art show. There are numerous other art-related programs throughout the year.

The city of Hoover has continued to contribute greatly to the ever-growing needs of the gardens. In 2007, they constructed a building to house our horticulturist and serve as a storage room for our tools, golf carts, and charging station. The city has also added office space in what was once the garage area. Future plans include an education and environmental center along with an intergenerational garden that will encompass the whole property; these new features will make possible more learning experiences for both children and adults.

Sculptural adornment has not been lacking in our gardens either. Three wonderful bronze sculptures have been donated. The first, a large figure of a tortoise pulling a hare in a wagon, was donated by the Bluff Park Art Association. This one seems to be the most popular with children. Close by is another bronze hare in a sitting position holding a cane. Aptly called "Waiting for a Ride," this piece was a gift of Michael and Deborah Stephens in honor of William and Claudett Billingsley. Another favorite sculpture, donated by Mr. and Mrs. Bob Smith to honor their grandchildren, Michael, Drew, Mary Kate, Gracie, Abby, and Emmy, features a mother duck walking to the lake with her ducklings. All of these works by renowned local artist Frank Fleming create a great deal of interest at the gardens.

In 2005, our first director retired and Larry Quick, a retired extension agent and education coordinator at Jefferson State Junior College, took over the job. Larry was already on our board as a volunteer and when his retirement from his extension job was imminent, the board knew this was a great opportunity for us. Under his leadership, things continue to progress very well at the gardens.

Cultivating Interns

Cindy Roodhouse Banach, Horticulturist.

Both of my parents were schoolteachers. Firm believers in education, they taught me a strong work ethic as I grew by their sides learning the nursery business. They inspired me to dream of one day creating a public garden, and they inspired me to help others follow the path I had taken by creating an intern program at the garden. Giving young people seeking a career in horticulture a chance to work on our grounds would be a benefit to them and to the gardens as well. Kay and I asked the board

Intern Ben Cleveland.

to approve of this new program and planned to fund it into the future.

The program began in 2003, and we have had wonderful interns ever since. One of our earliest interns, Cindy Roodhouse Banach, has since moved up to become our director of horticulture. Another hard-working young man, Ben Cleveland, has

been awarded a scholarship to study ornamental horticulture at Auburn University.

We have thus far had about a dozen interns working with us through this program. They came to us from a variety of schools, and two of them were homeschooled. Our most recent intern, Macie Brown, is a UAB biology graduate who plans to pursue additional education. Most of our interns were referred to the gardens by other students.

The Voices of Children

Perhaps the most rewarding aspect of daily life at Aldridge Gardens is seeing the great number of children who participate in programs here. Soon after we opened to the public in 2002, Dr. Vasha Rosenblum, a retired teacher and specialist in early childhood education from the Hoover school system, developed a children's learning garden on the farthermost north side of the property. Dr. Rosenblum applied for a grant for this purpose and once the grant was received, she was hired as education

Dr. Vasha Rosenblum.

Colleen Bedics, the current Education Director.

coordinator for the gardens. She applied for and obtained numerous grants to develop programs to teach the basics of gardening, vermiculture, and the planting of geometric beds for vegetables, flowers, and other crops. The geometric beds are

The Field Trip Garden

intended to provide math lessons to the children. Dr. Rosenblum retired from this position in 2006, but continues to work as a volunteer on our children's area, called the Field Trip Garden.

Our children's programs operate year-round and serve students at schools throughout our region. There is an immense amount of planning and coordination that requires the hard work of the entire gardens' staff under the leadership of Director Larry Quick. We are grateful to all of our staff members for these successful programs. We have received many colorful letters from participating children, including pictures describing what they have learned at the gardens. One special teacher, Clark Underbakke, sends us a booklet with pictures from his class every year. We treasure every one of these pictures and letters.

Mr. Clark Underbakke with a second grade class from Trace Crossings Elementary School in Hoover.

Kay's Woodland Stream with some of the original 13 Snowflakes rooted in 1971.

Scouts in the Gardens

Throughout all the years that Kay and I lived on the property, we often allowed scout troops to enjoy retreats there. Now we reap the benefits of their presence on a regular basis in the form of the many projects they plan and carry out for us.

We now have a bird blind next to the trail to the dam and a scout trail on the south side of the property with a lookout over the lake. Another project continued that trail with steps made with crossties down to the main trail. Our most recent scout project is a stairway from the picnic area next to the lake up to the main walking trail. This one is built from treated lumber squares and filled with the same red rock that was used on the trail around the lake.

These wonderful additions to the gardens have thus far been carried out by Eagle Scouts. In each case, scout leaders from throughout the region have come to our director, Larry Quick, to decide on projects that would benefit the gardens and that are attainable by the young scouts.

Eagle Scout projects

One of many bluebird houses installed by Dr. Dan Holliman.

On the Trail of Birds

Bird Watching is one of the greatest recreations in our country, and we are proud to be a part of this wonderful hobby, thanks especially to Dr. Dan Holliman. A retired natural biologist from Birmingham-Southern College, where he had taught for almost forty years, Dr. Holliman first came to the gardens when he was searching for a place to rehabilitate a knee after an operation. He discovered our walking trails and began to observe the extensive bird life and mammal population on the grounds. He recognized that the gardens, with its rich plant life offering nesting grounds and its lake, offered a great sanctuary for wildlife.

Dr. Holliman's involvement with the gardens increased, and in 2006 he installed bluebird houses throughout the gardens in an attempt to increase their nesting habitat. By the end of that season the houses were filled, not only with bluebirds, but also with chickadees, nuthatches, and other birds. He began to identify the many bird species that migrate to and from our property, and later he tracked the kinds of mammals that live here. We now have a brochure that he developed for us in which all these bird and mammal species are listed; in it is pictured the bird trail that he mapped out. In gratitude to Dr. Holliman, we dedicated this bird trail in his name last year.

Our Treasured Volunteers

One key to the continued success of our gardens has to be our dedicated troop of volunteers. Their time and effort make everything good happen in the gardens, including so much that the yearly budget would simply not support. To watch the work of these dedicated people is to be overwhelmed by their commitment. They do everything from gate duty, to working in the house during our many events, to performing hard manual work on the property. Besides all the benefits they bring to the gardens, they are often the best spokespeople for what we represent as well. We are ever grateful to them.

Laverne Martin is in charge of our troop of volunteers. She consults with Director Larry Quick to assess the daily needs of the gardens, then coordinates a complicated schedule of tasks and workers. She has done this for us for a long time and does a wonderful job managing over 200 volunteers.

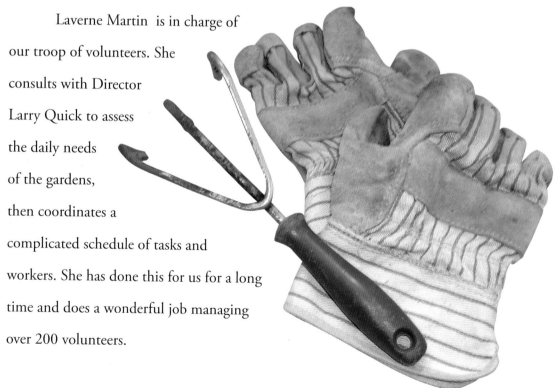

Some Very Special Trees

In addition to the story of the two magnolias I first planted for Mrs. Coxe on this property in 1966, there are interesting stories about three other trees that are special to the gardens today. The first story is about the beautiful gingko in front of the house. When I first bought the property, I asked Mrs. Coxe why this gingko was planted close to the edge of the circle in front of the home. She told me that previous owners of the property once had a home on the same spot where the house was built and that they had dug a well in the center of the circle. The builder of the Coxe home had capped the well with large

Gingko tree in the Fall.

crossties and topped them with metal. I noticed that the grass where the well was capped would always begin to wither during dry periods. When curiosity got the better of me, I dug down to where I thought the well was located and, sure enough, found the metal covering, and below it the crossties. When I dropped a small rock through the gap in the crossties, a second or two later I heard a splash. The well was indeed there. This explained why that gingko was offset when it was planted in the 1960s. Mrs. Coxe also remembered that her landscape architect, Edwin Jolly, had had Fraser Nursery in Birmingham plant this very unusual male gingko. The tree still

Small Redwood Tree at the pool.

stands in its original location.

Another tree story involved a special Japanese maple that, unlike the gingko, was moved many times before finding a final resting place. After my military service in the 1950s, I built a small house on Guntersville Lake. I wanted a special tree to plant next to this house, so one day I visited the old Fraser Nursery and found what I thought was the most beautiful tree I had ever seen. This maple had likely come directly from Japan because these trees were rare in the United States in the fifties. I planted the maple next to my little house. Several years later, when I bought a small house on 21st Avenue South next to our garden center in Birmingham, I decided to move the Japanese maple so that I could enjoy seeing it every day. In the late 1960s, I bought another home in Bluff Park and moved the maple to that location on Shades Crest Road. After several years in this home, I sold the property and moved back to 21st Avenue South; along with me came the maple where it was planted at our garden center. When I bought Mrs. Coxe's acreage in Hoover, I replanted the maple and thought the tree had finally found its permanent location. Once we opened the gardens to the public, however, board member John Floyd thought that the tree was too close to another maple and suggested that we move it to another location. The tree it was too close to was also special to me; it was one of ten Japanese maples that my father had grown from seed and planted in the 1960s. All of these maples still stand in the gardens today.

John Floyd selected an appropriate spot in the gardens for my special tree and we had a landscaping crew dig it up. This time, the tree's sixth move, we had to pay $3,900 for the process. A motorized crane was used to move the tree to its new location and a carpet of plywood boards had to be laid in front of the crane to avoid ruining the yard. I am convinced that this must be the most well-traveled Japanese maple in America. Needless to say, this tree is very special to me, and somehow I think it is very special to the gardens.

Eddie with the Japanese Maple.

Another treasured tree in the gardens is a rare tree from China, Metasequoia glyptostroboides or dawn redwood, which I planted next to the swimming pool around 1982. This redwood is deciduous, and by the late 1980s, Kay kept telling me that we should move the tree because its needles were always blowing into the pool. The tree had grown quite large so I knew I could not dig up the tree by hand. I decided to bring our Bobcat loader with a digger on the front from the Bessemer farm. After selecting a new location on the other side of the house, then digging a hole large enough to receive the tree, we proceeded to dig up the redwood. This was after Christmas and the tree was dormant. We dug for half a day, and when we finished, the roots were mutilated so badly that I thought the tree had little chance

Eddie with the Redwood Tree, Metasequoia Glytostroboides "Dawn Redwood".

of recovering. We continued anyway, and to this day Kay recalls the sight of our dragging this huge tree across the yard to its new home. Once planted, we had to tie the tree with big ropes to stakes in the ground. The tree survived. Then in 2002, when our landscape company hauled in tons of rock to install the waterfall, we almost lost the tree again. It has since recovered fully, and now we are fortunate enough to have a twelve-foot seedling that came up about fifteen feet from the mother tree.

Boathouse and the original magnolias that were planted by Eddie in 1966 when he first visited the property.

A Garden of Gifts

*t*he story of Aldridge Gardens is above all a history of gift-giving, beginning with the original gift of property that we made in memory of my wonderful parents and my late brother, Loren. Elizabeth and Tony Tanner made a large gift dedicated to their mothers, Martha Crabb and Cleo Tanner. Gene Smith, city councilman, and his wife, Pam, gave the gift of the frog pond in memory of his mother, Elaine Baird Smith. Friends of Dr. Charles Money gave the gift of the Saracenia Garden in his memory. Friends of the American Hydrangea Society in Atlanta, the

Kay's Woodland Stream.

Mid-South Hydrangea Society in Memphis, and the American Hydrangea Society of Birmingham gave gifts for a plaque in memory of Penny McHenry, who was

Penny McHenry Hydrangea.

founder of the American Hydrangea Society and later was instrumental in founding the Alabama Hydrangea Society. The Coral Bark Japanese maple in the pot at the entrance to the home was given in memory of Mrs. Jessie Numnum. The lacebark elm (Ulmus parvifolia) 'Allee', a large elm growing to the right of the circle in front of the house was given in memory of Lindsay Bates, whose mother, Beverly Bates, is a valued employee of the gardens. The Hugh Kaul Foundation has also made a large gift to the garden in memory of Bobbe Kaul, who had a consuming affection for all that grows. The Susan Mott Webb and the Robert Meyer Foundations have given very significant contributions to the gardens over the years as well as the Alabama Power Foundation, the Agee Foundation, and the Community Foundation of Greater Birmingham. These and all memorial gifts will be part of the gardens forever and will always be appreciated.

Lindsay Bates tree.

Jessie Numnum tree.

SHADE GARDEN

A mother's love is unconditional
She is at our side to nurture and comfort us
She encourages and supports us.
Take your time and reflect on life
In this garden dedicated to
Our mothers,

Martha Crabb & Cleo Tanner

"Come Along"
By Frank Fleming

A Gift of Bob and Alice Smith
In Honor of Their Grandchildren:
Michael, Drew, Mary Kate,
Gracie, Abby and Emmy

Ulmus parvifolia
Lacebark Elm "Allee"

In Memory of
LINDSAY KATHERINE BATES

Daughter of Jim & Beverly Bates

"On My Pond"
Look at the grass all around me
It's green as the smile on my face
Look at the trees they astound me
Wow, what a beautiful place
Kermit the Frog

In Loving Memory of
Elaine Baird Smith

Arbor Garden

In loving memory of Bobbe Kaul
who had consuming affection
for all that grows.
The Hugh Kaul Foundation

Bog Garden

Donated by
Friends of
Dr. Charles Money.

Lake Trail

A Gift of

Southern Progress Corporation

Building a Membership and Growing the Gardens

After six years of operation, our members number around 1,000—a relatively modest number. Fees collected from our membership help with the operation expenses, adding to the yearly contribution made by the city of Hoover. Fund-raising efforts and the many events held at the gardens also help with expenses. There are many expenses associated with operating the garden. Presently, entrance to the gardens is free. We are doing many things to help raise operating capital. Among these are weddings, Arts Alfresco in the gardens as well as horticultural events in the

Art in the Garden.

home and pavilion. We have "Hydrangeas Under the Stars" seated dinner events every year as well as plant sales in the spring and fall. We also rent the house and pavilion for business meetings. We have two Art Shows on the grounds every year that help with revenues. We also have outright donors every year that just give to the gardens. We still fall short on operating and I think the one thing that would offset this shortage would be to increase membership. Nevertheless, costs for payroll and

maintenance and grounds grow and we possibility charge a modest Obviously membership crucial part of picture.

of the home continue to now face the of having to entrance fee. building a larger seems to be a the financial

As we the gardens' are more and that we need a on the grounds

discuss building membership, we more convinced new building to increase

the number of education events we could offer. The idea of thus expanding the gardens has been the subject of much discussion, not just on our board but among the general public as well. Recently a woman wrote a letter to the Birmingham

News, expressing her opinion of our expansion plans. She praised the beauty of the woodland trails, the quiet atmosphere, the sparkling lake, and glimpses of wildlife; and she worried that the serenity of this natural sanctuary in the heart of Hoover might be easily destroyed by expansion. She said that there were few places left within easy reach where one could "simply relax and enjoy a little time" far from the maddening crowd.

This reader's opinion had a profound effect on me. I agreed totally that our main goal had to be preserving the natural sanctuary of the gardens. This has, after all, been the purpose of the gardens from the very beginning. Nevertheless, we believe that a new educational and environmental building and a new intergenerational garden will enrich our visitors' experience of the gardens, and in no way harm that experience. We hope that our totally green (Leadership in Energy and Environment Design or LEED-approved) building will blend in with the existing natural sanctuary.

There are many needs for a building like this in the gardens. More space would be available for children's programs, horticultural group meetings, an auditorium for lectures, offices for employees and the director, and possibly a garden-type restaurant. The new building would help relieve overuse of the home, which has long since provided a wonderful venue for weddings and other happy events. Along with the education and environmental center, we would like to add an amphitheater overlooking the lake. We hope that this increased potential in our gardens would encourage new membership, essential to helping pay our expenses. In planning for growth of the gardens, I am often reminded of my father who often cautioned me

to "leave well enough alone" whenever I became overly ambitious about something I wanted to do in the business. But I am also reminded of my mother's philosophy that "there is always room for improvement." As we strive for this improvement, our basic goal, to preserve the beauty and serenity of the gardens, will always be our first one.

A Garden for All Ages

When the original master plan for the gardens was drawn up, it called for a children's garden in one area of the property. We formed a committee and agreed to hire Cindy Tyler from Terra Designs in Pittsburgh, Pennsylvania, to develop a specific plan for a children's garden. The committee met with Cindy Tyler in a three-day workshop to explore the idea. It soon became evident to the committee that with the gardens covering only thirty acres, it would be difficult to designate a specific spot for a children's garden.

Alan and Claudia McGill.

One of our committee members, Catherine Hall, a marketing executive from Southern Living, suggested that we consider an intergenerational garden instead. While this idea has not yet been fully developed, it would encompass the whole garden instead of one smaller area. The idea is to involve children, parents, and grandparents and retain the wonderful woodland setting we already have. In many ways, we are already an intergenerational garden, with the sculptures, children's learning garden, water features, trails, picnic area, lake, and other features.

A Fruitful Retirement

Once Kay and I retired from our family business, back in 1999, we enjoyed many years of traveling, mainly to gardens in the U.S., Canada, New Zealand, Australia, and Europe. Callaway Gardens in Pine Mountain, Georgia, is special to us because it was where we spent our honeymoon 27 years ago. In addition, I served two terms on the board at the Birmingham Botanical Gardens, served on the board at Aldridge Gardens since 1997, and spoke often at garden clubs, civic groups, and various associations. The eight years I served on the board at the Birmingham Botanical Gardens was a great experience for me. We have made lasting friendships with

Kay and Eddie with Mr. Bo Callaway in 2008 at the Callaway Gardens Chapel.

the people associated with this world-class garden and our hope for the future is that both gardens will continue the good relationship we have today. We personally support both gardens, as do so many in our community. Retirement also brought me the joy of working in our own yard. It's certainly nice to make whatever changes I like there without going through a committee.

A Dream Fulfilled

When I reflect back on the beginning of Aldridge Gardens, I realize that the lupus that struck me in the middle of my life created a sense of urgency that propelled me to get the garden going as soon as possible. I was not sure how long I would be around. It has now been thirty years since I bought the Hoover property and a full twelve years since we formed the charitable trust with the city to begin the gardens. Kay and I look back on the wonderful eighteen years we lived on the property, but we agree that our greatest pleasure and satisfaction began with the trust and the beginning of the gardens. Originally, our gardens were called Aldridge Park and Gardens, later changed to Aldridge Gardens, and most recently renamed Aldridge Botanical Gardens. Kay and I decided that any of these names were fine with us.

Never in our wildest dreams could we have foreseen that twelve years after the trust, we would see more than 75,000 visitors to the gardens. We are constantly overwhelmed by the number of weddings, arts activities, educational programs, daily walkers and picnickers. Like our many visitors, Kay and I now enjoy the property much more than during the busy years we lived there when we were working long hours at our business across town. Remembering my leap of faith in buying the Hoover property, my father's suggestion of someday making it into a public garden, and seeing that dream fulfilled has filled my heart with gratitude and the sense that I have truly fulfilled my own destiny. We believe the future of the gardens will be determined by destiny.

The emerging sepals of Snowflake Hydrangea.

*A Trail Map
of Aldridge Gardens*

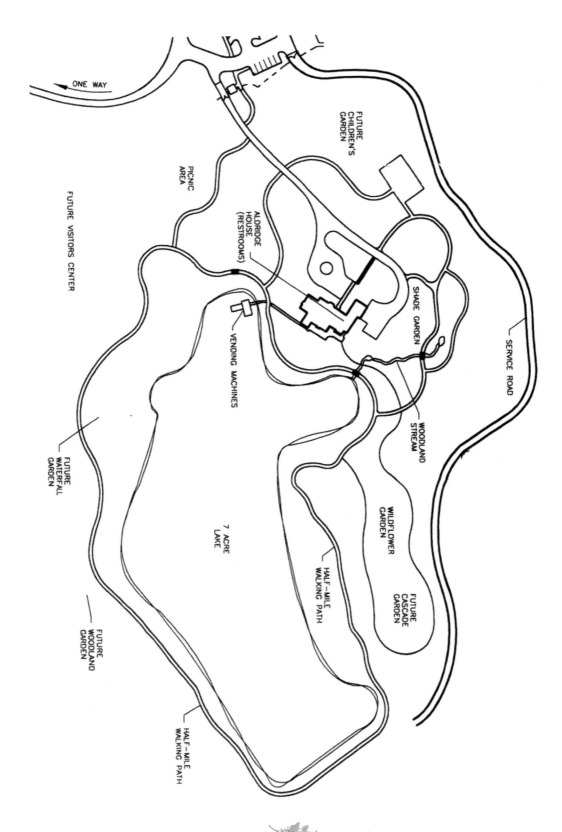

ONE WAY

FUTURE CHILDREN'S GARDEN

PICNIC AREA

FUTURE VISITORS CENTER

ALDRIDGE HOUSE (RESTROOMS)

VENDING MACHINES

SHADE GARDEN

SERVICE ROAD

WOODLAND STREAM

FUTURE WATERFALL GARDEN

7 ACRE LAKE

WILDFLOWER GARDEN

FUTURE CASCADE GARDEN

HALF-MILE WALKING PATH

FUTURE WOODLAND GARDEN

HALF-MILE WALKING PATH

Aerial photo of Aldridge Gardens, 2003.